W9-AXT-486

GREAT CARS

Above: The three-wheeler was an economy car popular in Britain and Europe before the First World War. It paid a lower road tax than cars with four wheels. Best known was the Morgan, made in Malvern Link in England from 1909. The 1933 version pictured here was quite fast, with a powerful 2-cylinder vee-engine and chain drive.

Overleaf: The magnificent 1934 V-12 cylinder form Hispano Suiza luxury car. Originally from Spain, the make was later based in France. These fine motorcars were fitted with the very best body styles by famous coachbuilders.

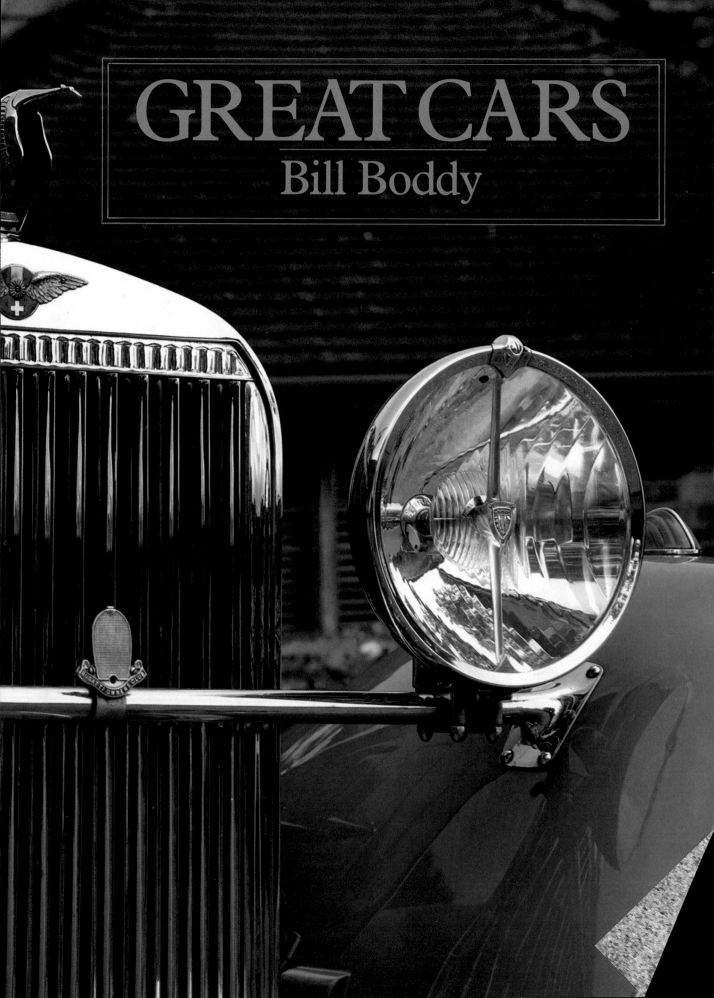

GREAT CARS

Bill Boddy

Contents

Left: The Italian Maserati – originally the ideal of the brothers of that name and a car to rival the Ferrari for speed and exciting performance. The classic example shown here was built in 1955. In the background there is a distinctly different car – a 1920s French 5 hp Citroën.

This book was devised and produced by
Multimedia Publications (UK) Ltd

Editor **Richard Rosenfeld**
Design **Behram Kapadia**
Picture Research **Anne Usbourne**
Production **Arnon Orbach**

Copyright © Multimedia Publications (UK) Ltd 1984

All rights reserved. No part of this book may be reproduced or transmitted in any form or by means, electronic or mechanical, including photocopying, recording, or by any information storage and retrieval system, without permission in writing from the publisher.

ISBN 0-8317-9179-9

First published in the United States of America 1984 by Gallery Books, an imprint of W. H. Smith Publishers Inc., 112 Madison Avenue, New York, NY 10016

Originated by D S Colour International Ltd, London
Typeset by Rowland Phototypesetting (London) Ltd
Printed in Spain by Cayfosa, Barcelona
Dep. Legal B-28.965 - 1984

Introduction

Historians differ as to when the first motorcar – the original "horseless carriage" – was made, but by 1896 Benz certainly had a practical petrol-burning vehicle on the roads of Germany.

By the turn of the century it was possible to buy motorcars from makers such as Benz, Panhard-Levassor, Peugeot and others. They were primitive – difficult to start and then to keep going – but dogged, mechanically minded owners did get some sense out of them. These early cars terrified the horses they were eventually to supersede!

France was quick to develop its motor industry, while in Britain Knight, the talented Lanchester brothers, and the Daimler company in Coventry were also early on the scene with petrol cars. Steam and electricity were sometimes used as motive power, the latter for silent, odorless town carriages.

Built for speed
The first motor races were organized in France, on the long, ruler-straight *routes nationales* down which Napoleon's armies had once marched. In view of the untried nature of the competing vehicles it is surprising that these races were held over very long distances, along dusty, unguarded public highways.

The Paris-Vienna, Paris-Bordeaux-Paris and Paris-Berlin races – over hundreds, even thousands, of kilometers – made people realize that reliable, fast cars did exist, and could possibly rival trains as one of the most efficient forms of transport.

Opening up the Prairies
By 1905/7 the motorcar was in considerable demand, and reliable enough to be used by doctors and traveling salesmen. In America the ingenious two-speed, transversely sprung Model-T Ford, introduced in 1907, opened up the Prairies as never before and by 1927 over 15 million had been sold.

Today, there are millions of cars all over the world. Almost ten million are produced in the States each year with Ford alone being responsible for nearly two million of that number. The car is one of the lynch-pins of modern society and this book celebrates the greatest of them.

Left: Pioneer among the world's car manufacturers, Panhard-Levassor of France established the standard form of front engine and rear wheel drive, with a "crash" gearbox.

Edwardians

In the early 1900s King Edward's interest in Daimlers did much to make cars more generally accepted. They were still the preserve of the wealthy, used for attending sporting and social occasions, but were fast becoming more practical and better suited to everyday travel. Vintage cars produced between 1905 and 1918 are classed today as Edwardians.

The Silver Ghost

This was a period of consolidation for the automobile, when engines of considerable power were first used to propel beautifully appointed and finished closed carriages. They were smooth and quiet. Most famous of these cars was the celebrated 40/50 hp Rolls-Royce Silver Ghost of 1907 which soon became universally accepted as the best car in the world.

Such motorcars, usually driven by chauffeurs, were used for long-distance tours across Europe, even though the tyres did not last very long and were extremely costly to replace.

Smaller cars, such as the single-cylinder Swift and the Austin Seven, were much less expensive, and therefore very popular. A similar mass-produced, competitively priced American car of the same period was the all black Model-T Ford from Detroit.

Hitting 100 mph

In the Edwardian period, racing cars became about as fast as their drivers and their tyres could cope with. Even Mercedes, which specialized in luxury rather than sports cars, designed a winner – the very powerful Mercedes Sixty, which won the 1903 Gordon Bennet race held in Ireland. Road racing, now held over policed, closed circuits, continued to advance the science of fast motoring so that by the time Brooklands Track in Surrey, England, was opened in 1907, racing projectiles could exceed 100 mph. An American steam car, the Stanley, had been timed at 121.57 mph in 1906 on the beach at Daytona, Florida. The motorcar's place was now firmly established.

Left: The Napier was one of the first 6-cylinder cars, built in Acton, London. The 60 hp example shown took the 24-hour record at Brooklands in 1907.

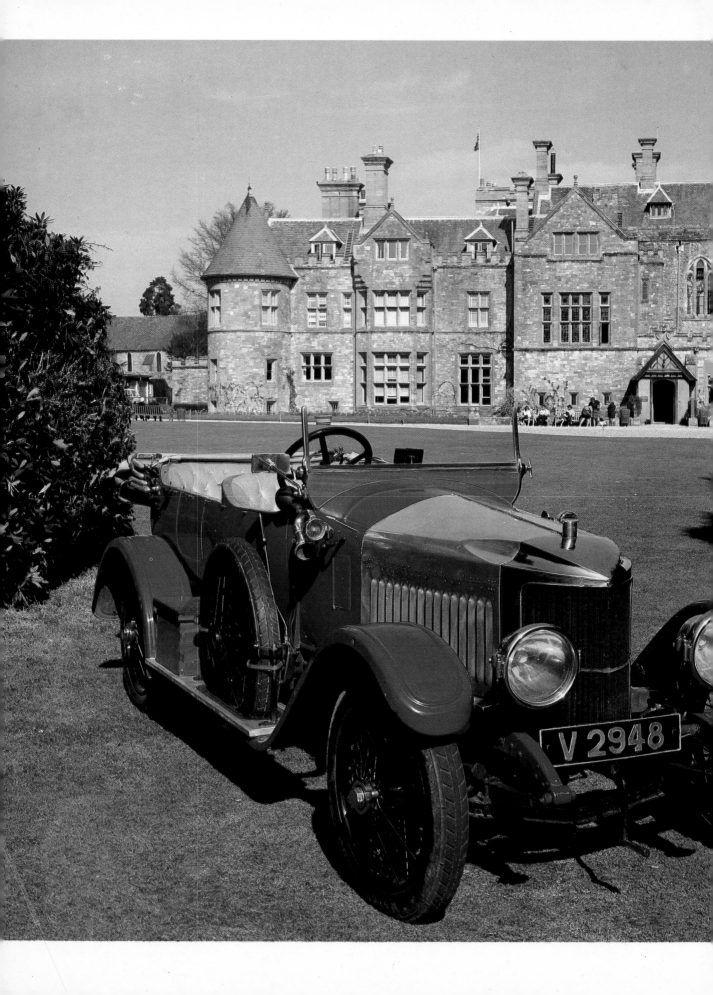

Above: The Series-B Bear-Cat of 1913 was a sports car, with just two exposed bucket-type seats and the spare tyre strapped on behind. A grand way of overtaking horse-drawn vehicles, with the wind howling round the occupants' heads battling with the snarl of the exhaust.

Top: The most famous of British cars, the 40/50 hp Rolls-Royce, was quickly christened "The Best Car in the World". This is the original example of the great 40/50, the Silver Ghost of 1907 that, under official observation, accomplished a 15 000-mile trial with only one stop – the petrol tap had closed – and afterwards needed very few repairs.

Left: The Prince Henry Vauxhall of 1914, a British sporting motorcar which gained the Luton Company much fame. It was the forerunner of the immortal 30/98 Vauxhall fast-tourer. The engine was quite unexciting to look at, with one carburetor and the valves at the side, but it gave a top speed of approximately 70 mph.

11

Left: This is a rather rare make of car, built by the Vulcan Iron Works in 1908. The touring body is typical of the period, with a large hood to cover all the seats, a high plate-glass windscreen and artillery-type wheels. The lamps would be a mixture of gas and oil lighting.

Below: The British Daimler was another touring car, made only a little later than the Vulcan. It had a modest top speed of 15 hp, and had just adopted sleeve valves by 1910, in contrast to the up-and-down camshaft operated poppet valves of most other cars. The make was easily recognised by its fluted radiator.

Above: The production or
catalogue edition of the original
1907 Silver Ghost. Note the
hood straps, the "button"
leather seats, the herring-bone
pattern Dunlop tyres and the
big, gas headlamps.

Right: One of the more exciting
cars to own in the days prior to
the First World War was this
15.9 hp Hispano-Suiza, a
favourite car of the King of
Spain, and therefore known as
the Alphonso model. This
white tourer is owned by the
Beaulieu Motor Museum.

Left: The Rolls-Royce Silver Ghost was made from 1907 until 1925. The basic design did not change much, although many improvements were introduced. This one, finished just before Europe went to war with Germany in 1914, has a German made Schebera-Shapiro body.

Right: Not all motorcars were driven by petrol engines in the early days of road transport. Some people found that type of engine noisy, smelly and difficult to start. The electric automobile like this 1914 Detroit Electric coupé was noiseless and moved off at the flick of a switch but soon ran out of power.

Left: A superb 1909 Rolls-Royce, the work of that great and humble engineer Mr – later Sir – Henry Royce.

Right: The Cadillac became one of the finest of American automobiles. The Model-A Cadillac of 1903 offered reliability at low cost, using a single-cylinder engine.

Above: The powerful Rolls-Royce, even in Edwardian days, was well capable of carrying comfortable, even luxurious, closed bodywork, like this yellow rounded-back limousine of 1910, with its aluminum bonnet. The elegance, apart from the flowing lines of the coachwork, is set off by the carriage style side lamps – a throw back to the horse-drawn age – and the very large electric headlamps. Note the "Spirit of Ecstasy" mascot on the radiator cap, without which no Rolls-Royce is complete.

Above: Before the First World War young American sportsmen used to like to drive about in automobiles that would show the dust to their more staid elders. One such was the Mercer, racy in appearance and performance. This is the Series-J Raceabout of 1913, which was sometimes fitted with a circular windshield on the steering wheel, which turned with it to protect the intrepid driver from the wind!

Above: A serious rival to the Rolls-Royce in the "Best Car" stakes, or so its sponsor thought, was the Sheffield-Simplex. It was so powerful that it required only two forward gears. It did not last long in production.

Vintage Years

The vintage years ran from 1919 to 1930. It is one of the most interesting of all in terms of motorcar development and usage. After the war, many people had war gratuities to spend but money was limited, even if petrol, tyres and other motoring needs were comparatively cheap. So for a time the crude "stick-and-string" motorcycle-engined cyclecars, which had burst upon the world in 1912, resurfaced, although soon to be replaced by small cars such as the immortal Austin Seven.

The Austin baby was followed by the Singer Junior, Morris Minor and – smartly styled from Ford's Dagenham plant in England – the Ford Eight, which became the first £100 saloon. Interim two-cylinder small cars, such as the Rover Eight and Stoneleigh, perished before the onslaught of more sophisticated "baby-cars". However, the twin-cylinder Jowett from Bradford and the three-wheeled Morgan from Malvern survived.

Vintage sportscars

The vintage era was notable for some very fine sports cars, including the improved overhead valved 30/98 Vauxhall and the great 3-litre and 4½-litre, overhead camshaft 16-valve Bentleys in England, or the Stutz, Duesenberg and Chrysler in America. The French Bugatti and Italian Alfa Romeo also gained their name in this exciting time.

Motor racing was very much to the fore, with the annual Indianapolis 500 in the USA, and road races held almost everywhere on the European Continent.

Engine sizes in Grand Prix racing were continually being reduced for safety and cost reasons, but nevertheless racing cars became ever quicker.

Greater sophistication

Cars still had separate chassis frames and usually leaf road springs, as used on carts, but from 1924 front-wheel brakes had appeared, even on many cheap automobiles, and multi-cylinder power units were in fashion. The market was flooded with masses of makes, of which only a handful survived, and the owner-driver was fast replacing the professional chauffeur. Saloon bodies, often made of fabric for low weight and cheapness, together with Triplexis, shatter-proof "safety" glass, were introduced.

Tyres were less likely to puncture and lasted longer, and large "balloon" tyres had arrived by the mid-1920s. Self-starters and crude windscreen wipers added to motoring's sophistication.

Left: The interior of a 1925 Rolls-Royce with its walnut dashboard.

Left: Englishmen love sports cars and in 1927 one of the best of the smaller engined ones was this 1½-litre Alvis 12/50, made in Coventry. It had a beetle-backed body.

Right: Glorious in every way and certainly one of the "Greats" of motoring, America's Model-J Duesenberg had a straight eight-cylinder twin overhead camshaft motor, said to develop 265 hp in supercharged form. The fenders and side-mounted spare wheels of this 1930 model are of typical American design.

Below: German might is personified in this enormous 110 mph 36/220 hp Mercedes Benz. It had a supercharger controlled by the accelerator and always wore three outside flexible exhaust pipes and the Mercedes "triple-star" mascot.

Left: The Frazer Nash rivalled Alvis on British roads in the 1920s. It was a lightweight car with various engines for different models. At this time all had a chain transmission instead of a sliding-pinion gearbox, which saved weight and made gear shifting easy.

The model pictured here had a side-valve 1½-litre Anzani or Powerplus engine and the doorless body was made of aluminum, again to save weight. The car's manufacturer, Capt. Archie Frazer-Nash, used to say that if his customers could drive his cars properly they would be athletic enough to jump in over the sides – so doors, which would have cost more money, were unnecessary!

Right: At one time all cheap American tourers looked alike. The Doge Brothers' car was no exception. But this one, with its bright paintwork instead of the usual all-black finish, was the first sign of change.

Right: Among the three contenders for the title of best American automobile was the Cadillac, which in its exotic V-16 cylinder form took some beating. At the time Rolls-Royce had just 6 cylinders and 12 was regarded as a luxury.

Left: Moving up in size from the Alvis and Frazer-Nash, one of the greatest and most famous British sports cars before the War was the Bentley. This 4½-litre model had an engine of the same mechanical kind as the original 3-litre Bentley and was given more power by means of a huge Villiers supercharger, seen poking out in front.

Right: A fascinating rear view of one of the great 4½-litre Bentleys. It shows the rear petrol tank with its quick-action filler cap, the boat-tail body with windscreens for the passengers in the back, and the fold-down front windscreen, with "aero" screens to use when it was folded.

Left: This dramatic SSK Mercedes Benz was typical of the big performance cars produced by the German firm.

Overleaf: After the pre-war Bearcat, the American Stutz developed into a still quick but more civilized car. It used a low-slung "safety" chassis and derived its speed from an in-line 8-cylinder engine with single or twin overhead camshaft valve-gear. Shown here is a 1929 Black Hawk.

Left: The last of the magnificent Bentleys made and designed by Walter Bentley was the 6-cylinder, 8-litre version. It could exceed 100 mph with a closed saloon body. The one seen here has a sports-saloon body by Mulliner's and it was this Bentley which so frightened Rolls-Royce Ltd that they bought Bentley out!

Right: Biggest car in the world, wheels and tyres included, was this astonishing Bugatti Royale, which the eccentric Ettore Bugatti intended for kings and other heads of state. It used a 12-litre, 8-cylinder engine coupled to a two-speed back axle.

Left: Beneath the bonnet of a non-supercharged racing Bentley, which had two carburetors. The shaft running down in front of them is the substantial steering column. Note the racing number on the side of the body and the bulge on the bonnet to clear one of two magnetos.

Right: The ultimate version of the "Royal Car", the Coventry-made Daimler, was the Double-Six 50. It was so called because it had a vee-arrangement of its 12 cylinders and was taxed in England as developing 50 hp. Its hallmarks were smoothness and hushed running.

Race for Power

The end of what is now known as the vintage period of motoring brought considerable change, both in the cars themselves and the conditions under which they were used.

"Silent sports cars"

The American Ford V8 was a low-cost, speedy – almost too fast for its brakes and many of those who bought it! Rolls-Royce had managed to take over the old Bentley Company by 1931 and were making very refined, fast new Bentley "silent sports cars" at Derby, England, using Rolls-Royce parts.

The American Hudson straight-eight was revamped in Britain by the great automotive engineer Reid Railton as the Railton. It cost about a third as much as the new three-and-a-half-litre Rolls-Bentley, but matched it for speed and acceleration.

Those who still admired vintage cars, even though these were now some ten years old, disliked the new trends in styling, as seen in the later Jaguar-inspired SS90 and SS100. They also had doubts about the use of one-piece body and chassis construction, despite its lower costs and greater rigidity. In the opinion of the diehards, separate chassis frames withstood rusting better. But they deplored the low-geared steering and sometimes soggy suspension of some 1930s cars. For all that, car sales worldwide increased enormously, with private owners predominant. Petrol pumps had replaced the clumsy two-gallon petrol tins, tyres had new-found durability and cheap sports cars such as the MG Midget, Singer Nine and the improved four-speed Austin Sevens were available.

Light-weight power

On the motor racing front the prowess of Bugatti, Maserati and Alfa Romeo faded after 1934, as the Hitler-inspired teams of Mercedes Benz and Auto-Union Grand Prix racers, of light weight and fabulous power, dominated the road racing scene.

Raymond Mays obtained financial support for his one-and-a-half-litre ERA (English Racing Automobiles) racing cars, using supercharged Riley-based engines to challenge the Italian Maserati and French Bugatti cars in the *voiturette* field. By 1939 the land speed record was held by John Cobb's Napier twin-engined Railton at 369.7 mph, set at Bonneville, Utah.

Left: This stylish Duesenberg SJ was made in 1933, and features a beautiful two-seater body by Walton.

Left: After the Rolls-Royce 40/50 hp Silver Ghost came a modernized version, called the New Phantom, followed by this, the better-braked and sprung Phantom II. It had overhead instead of side-by-side valves, and revised springing.

Right: The Aston Martin was a complex but highly efficient British small sports car, seen here in 1934 "Le Mans" form. The engine oil was carried in the tank at the front.

Below: In the same year you could buy the smaller sporting Lagonda Rapier, which had a 1,100 cc 4-cylinder engine, of the racing twin-cam type. After Lagonda Motors dropped it, a separate company went on making it in London.

Above: Typically British, the big 4½-litre Invicta was notable in this form for its low chassis. It had a high-power 6-cylinder Meadows motor of simple design. This 1934 model has a Salmons coupé body. The open cars were known as 100 mph Invictas.

Top: A real breakaway in technique was seen in the 328 BMW from Germany, produced just before the war. It used soft springing that gave wonderful road-holding, and its high-power 6-cylinder engine incorporated specially efficient but simple valve gear. It used three carburetors.

Right: Citroën of Paris produced cars in enormous numbers, but in 1934 introduced the new front-wheel drive, torsion bar sprung Traction Avant. It brought new standards of safe, comfortable motoring to the masses.

Left: One of the most covetable pre-war sports cars, this Italian Tipo 8C 2300 Alfa Romeo from Milan was a race-bred sports car, with all the quick response and lively handling of a thoroughbred racehorse. It won many victories in the sports car races of the 1930s, and was driven in them by the world's most famous racing drivers, such as Nuvolari, Varzi, Earl Howe and Sir Henry Birkin.

The engine had eight cylinders in line, with a central drive for the twin overhead-camshafts and Rootes supercharging.

Below: The 8C Alfa Romeo engine. Note the ribbed inlet piping, the steering box and, sticking up at the top of the engine, the ignition distributor for all eight cylinders.

Above: How the fortunate driver and passenger would have seen the 8C Alfa Romeo. The back seats have a fabric cover.

Right: The splendid 1932 8C 2300 Alfa Romeo sports/racing car. The body is by Carrosieur. Certainly one of the Great Cars, the Alfa set remarkably high standards of road manners.

Above: A very rare British design for a very large, special sports car. The chassis is that of the Daimler Double-Six, much lowered, given a stylish coupé body by Corsica. Note the length of the bonnet!

Below: Rolls-Royce eventually entered the V-12 cylinder field with their 7.4-litre Phantom III. It had hydraulic valve clearance adjustment that had to be kept very clean and American-style independent springing for the front wheels.

Right: The stylish mascot of the luxury Packard V-12 cylinder.

Below: This is a one-off, 6-cylinder Speed-20 Alvis. It is based on the car it is thought Sir Henry Birkin would have raced instead of Bentleys and Maseratis, had he not died of blood poisoning before it was completed!

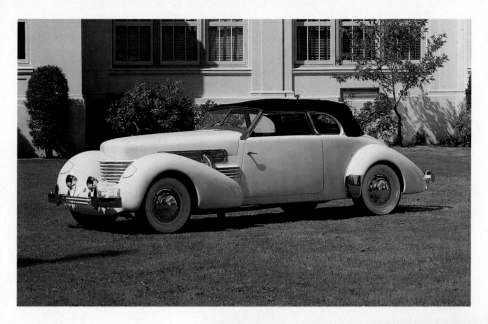

Left: The La Salle was the less costly version of the Packard range of cars, which were generally regarded as the best made cars in America.

Left: The Cord 812 is a very important American car because it used front-wheel drive, on Miller lines, for a handsome phaeton with electric gear selection.

Right: French style can be recognised in the lines of this Vanden Plas-bodied Type 135 Delahaye, a pioneer maker from the early days of motoring, although this one was built in 1939.

Left: The Packard was probably America's top car and this picture of a 1933 roadster says it all. The front bumper, or fender, and the whitewall tyres, are typically American. The radiator retained its characteristic shape almost to the end.

War Years

Automobile development in the 1940s was hampered by World War Two. The war restricted European motoring to essential purposes because petrol was heavily rationed. With headlamps masked and street lighting extinguished to make life more difficult for night bombers from Germany – and even signposts removed in Britain to hamper invaders – accurate map reading became essential!

Re-emergence of the greats
War vehicles superseded private cars, the production of which virtually ceased, only to recover slowly from 1947 onwards. However, the great cars had not been entirely eliminated. Jowett, with Gerry Palmer's ingenious flat four-engined torsion-suspended Javelin, and Armstrong Siddeley with their range of new cars, futuristically styled and with 2-litre, 6 cylinder engines, were among the first of a new breed of cars. They were easier to drive and maintain than ever before. Armstrong Siddeley named their cars after great aeroplanes of the war, for example as the Lancaster and Typhoon.

Dignified Rovers
The German Volkswagen "Beetle", rejected by the British as war reparations, was sold in fantastic numbers. Among a spate of tiny economy cars, the dignified and well conceived Rover family stood out, and Alvis went on making fine cars, led at first by the TA14.

MG, making mostly sports cars down at Abingdon, had a huge success with the TC and TD Midgets, the latter with the now popular independent front springing. However, Rolls-Royce and Bentley had yet to give up mechanical servo brakes, driven from the gearbox, not to mention the chassis frame.

Great motorcars were in the offing and this was certainly not a period of stagnation. Automatic transmissions came to Europe from America, although the manual gearbox still refuses to die, and it was left to the USA to fit screen washers as a standard item.

Unfortunately strikes slowed down post-war outputs in both Europe and America. Before the War automobile production ran at four-and-a-half million a year in the USA alone.

Left: American roads and freeways permitted very large and spacious automobiles, such as this 1948 Pontiac Silver Streak sedan, a General Motors product that was thought ugly in Europe.

Left: This post-war sports car was the idea of the famous rally driver Donald Healey who, in 1949, had to use available parts to build a saleable car. The engine was a 2½-litre inclined overhead valve Riley. Note the recessed headlamps, the "aero" screens – the main glass slid down into the scuttle for racing – and the large trailing arms of the independent front suspension.

Right: This 1950 Jaguar XK120 created a sensation when first introduced by Sir William Lyons. It was very fast, had eye-catching flowing lines, less good brakes at first, and the smooth twin-cam 3.4-litre Jaguar engine.

Below: Hard-sprung and brutally efficient, this post-war HRG used a Singer 1½-litre overhead-cam engine.

Above: A Detroit built car to rival the silence and quality of the British Rolls-Royce – the 1950 Series-62 Cadillac with a spacious four-door saloon, or sedan, body. The headlamps have now become part of the wings and substantial bumpers protect the body when parking.

Below: Called the "Standard of the World", by 1950 the Cadillac had gained more power and had grown tiny tail-fins to show it was not an Oldsmobile! The low roof and bow-fronted windshield helped to reduce aerodynamic drag on this two-door Series 50-61 coupé.

Right: From the early 1920s the General Motors Chevrolet tried to eat into Ford's sales. As a 6-cylinder competitor for the 4-cylinder Ford, it was noted for its longevity, earning the nickname "Cast-Iron Wonder" or the "Stove-bolt Six". In later times the inexpensive "Chevvy" retained these qualities, and the 1948 example shown here has a convertible body.

Above: The curious mascot on a 1950 Dodge Brothers' radiator cap.

Left: No one has really experienced motoring to the full who has not driven a 12-cylinder Ferrari, with its inimitable exhaust snarl and fine road-holding and cornering.

Above: After the war the British sports car, the Aston Martin, was made for a time by David Brown. This very impressive model is a 2½-litre DB2 coupé.

Left: One of the better known roadgoing Ferraris was the Type 166 Inter of 1947. While it retained all the Ferrari appeal, its body lines were not the prettiest available.

Right: The Chrysler, built by an American company independent of General Motors, made its name as an advanced, even sporting, auto before the war. It was continued afterwards, as a Buick competitor. With the side-valve engine in this 1948 model, it also has Chrysler's famed "Town & Country" convertible coachwork, with "woodie" styling.

Below: After the war Rolls-Royce needed rather smaller-engined cars than formerly and the Silver Wraith was the answer. It used 4.2-litre and 4.5-litre engines with the inlet valves overhead but the exhaust valves at the side of the cylinders. This one has a coupe-de-ville body, with flowing wings.

Left: This striking mascot was the elegant hallmark of a 1950s Packard.

Right: The exciting looking Healey sports car, with 2½-litre Riley inclined-valve engine, with its main windscreen erect.

Below: Although many American cars tended to look much like one another in the 1950s, as they had in the 1920s, this frontal view could be nothing but a Chevrolet.

New Designs

The decade after the 1940s saw great cars on the roads of the world again. The sleek Jaguar XK120 from Coventry, England, was the forerunner of the great Jaguar run of Le Mans winning sports cars, culminating in the very exciting 150 mph E-type. At first, however, Jaguar, like other British manufacturers, had to export 96 per cent of their output.

Build your own

Colin Chapman began the famous Lotus line with kit-cars you could assemble in your garage, which later included the classic Elite and Elan. The Rootes Group made good quality sports cars under the old Sunbeam and Talbot names, while glass fibre was seen as a way of eliminating the need for the extremely expensive body presses for forming the conventional steel bodywork. The Morgan Motor Company made its 4/4 and Plus-4 individualistic sports models by hand, and many new small concerns established a foothold on the automotive market.

Mercedes Benz were back, with impeccably engineered cars and the 3-litre Austin Healey 100 set a new fashion in strong, low-slung British sports cars. The rally world was in full cry, with the Monte Carlo Rally still popular, and motor racing was beginning to appeal to the ordinary person. The 300SL "Gull-Wing" Mercedes Benz set a fashion of its own.

Cars for royalty

From 1950 heads of state, led by HRH Queen Elizabeth II, the Shah of Persia and General Franco, traveled in the greatest comfort in the fabulous Rolls-Royce Phantom IV, of which only 16 were built. New concepts of appearance, allied to hushed fast running, were set by the Rolls-Royce engineered Bentley Continental. The pioneer make of Daimler produced new cars, having reverted to conventional poppet inlet and exhaust valves after a long spell with the oil-consuming sleeve-valves.

It was a time of much technical advancement, with cars that were ever more pleasant to drive and easier to service. Many makes fell out of production, however, although Austin and Morris were still well to the fore in Britain, fighting a sales battle with the American-orientated cars from Ford and Vauxhall.

The beautiful looking racing cars, such as the Maserati 250F and Alfa Romeo Alfettas, were reaching their peak, the forerunners of today's great Formula One racing cars.

Left: The Mercedes Benz 300 SL is one of the celebrated classic cars of all time. It is very fast and beautifully made with a frame of many small, steel tubes, enabling the doors to open upwards like gull wings.

Top: Millionaire Briggs Cunningham was very anxious to win the Le Mans 24-hour race in France, so he spent a fortune on his Cunningham, using Chrysler Hemi-head V8 motors. This is the road-version of the C3.

Above: Sober to look at, the Chrysler 300B of 1956 was the most powerful American car, poking out 355 hp from its 5.4-litre engine.

Right: The Ford Thunderbird was one of America's best-known "fun-cars". It was the brainchild of Henry Ford II and was designed by Lewis Crusoe. By using many stock parts, its price was kept down. Its legend lives on!

Above: The ultimate guise of the epoch-marking XK Jaguar was this handsome, sleek XKI 50S coupé. It now has a 250 hp engine and disc brakes to match its fierce performance.

Left: This is the DB2/4 Hatchback edition of the popular Aston Martin sports coupé. It used a W.O. Bentley designed twin-cam 6-cylinder engine, and was effective on the race tracks.

Below: Always a performance auto, and early to use overhead valves, the Buick was favoured by HRH the Prince of Wales before the War. This is the 1951 "Super" version.

Above: Post World War Two economy turned even Rolls-Royce to the pressed steel body, but for those wealthy enough it was still possible in 1959 to have individually-constructed coachwork on a Silver Wraith chassis, as this Mulliner saloon proves.

Left: Lovers of open-air driving have small choice today. But the very fast Jaguar XK150 was available with a drophead coupé body, enabling the driver to catch the scents of the countryside or sit in snug warmth when it rained or was cold.

Below: Fabulously fast in its day, the superbly stylish Jaguar XK120, made in 1951. The engine, designed by Bill Haynes, used twin-overhead-camshafts that ran quietly, unlike those in racing car engines.

Right: Using largely Ford components and powerful engines like the Ford Chrysler or Cadillac V-8, the English sportsman Sydney Allard sold cars bearing his name. They did outstandingly well in mud trials, international rallies, and even in racing. He drove them himself and won the celebrated Monte Carlo Rally outright.

Left: The rugged French Delahaye was the kind of car you associate with the Riviera and smartly dressed ladies. This 1938 Type 135MS drophead coupé would have been just the car.

Right: In 1931 Rolls-Royce bought out the Bentley Motors company, run then by diamond millionaire Woolf Barnato, because they thought the W.O. Bentley designed 100 mph, 8-litre Bentley saloon might affect their sales. They then used a chassis and engine from a small Rolls-Royce to produce their first "Silent Sports Car". After the war they continued to build Rolls-Royce derived Bentleys like this Mk VI with its all-steel saloon body.

Left: Lancia of Turin were always innovators and they hardly ever made a bad car. This 1951 2½-litre V-6 cylinder Aurelia had impeccable road manners and was full of character.

Right: The celebrated Mercedes Benz 300SL from Stuttgart in Germany, with its "Gull-Wing" doors closed. Note the famous triple-star badge, hallmark of the cars from Stuttgart, Germany.